www.providencebooks.net

Publisher Contact

Email:contact@providencebooks.net

Social media: facebook.com/providencebooks

Acknowledgements

The team at Providence Books would like to thank our friends, family, suppliers and customers for making our vision of creating the highest-quality books a reality. Thanks for purchasing and enjoy the quotes!

This page is intentionally left blank

This page is intentionally left blank

A good compromise, a good piece of legislation, is like a good sentence; or a good piece of music. Everybody can recognize it. They say, 'Huh. It works. It makes sense.'

Barack Obama

A mother deserves a day off to care for a sick child or sick parent without running into hardship - and you know what, a father does, too. It's time to do away with workplace policies that belong in a 'Mad Men' episode.

Barack Obama

After 2014, we will support a unified Afghanistan as it takes responsibility for its own future.

Barack Obama

After a century of striving, after a year of debate, after a historic vote, health care reform is no longer an unmet promise. It is the law of the land.

Barack Obama

Al Qaeda is still a threat. We cannot pretend somehow that because Barack Hussein Obama got elected as president, suddenly everything is going to be OK.

Barack Obama

All of us take offense to anyone who reaps the rewards of living in America without taking on the responsibilities of living in America. And undocumented immigrants who desperately want to embrace those responsibilities see little option but to remain in the shadows, or risk their families being torn apart.

Barack Obama

America and Islam are not exclusive and need not be in competition. Instead, they overlap, and share common principles of justice and progress, tolerance and the dignity of all human beings.

Barack Obama

America is the student who defies the odds to become the first in a family to go to college - the citizen who defies the cynics and goes out there and votes - the young person who comes out of the shadows to demand the right to dream. That's what America is about.

Barack Obama

America isn't Congress. America isn't Washington. America is the striving immigrant who starts a business, or the mom who works two low-wage jobs to give her kid a better life. America is the union leader and the CEO who put aside their differences to make the economy stronger.

Barack Obama

America thrived in the 20th century because we made high school free. We sent a generation to college. We cultivated the most educated workforce in the world.

Barack Obama

Americans... still believe in an America where anything's possible - they just don't think their leaders do.

Barack Obama

And I will do everything that I can as long as I am President of the United States to remind the American people that we are one nation under God, and we may call that God different names but we remain one nation.

Barack Obama

And so our goal on health care is, if we can get, instead of health care costs going up 6 percent a year, it's going up at the level of inflation, maybe just slightly above inflation, we've made huge progress. And by the way, that is the single most important thing we could do in terms of reducing our deficit. That's why we did it.

Barack Obama

And that means that no matter how we reform health care, we will keep this promise to the American people: If you like your doctor, you will be able to keep your doctor, period. If you like your health care plan, you'll be able to keep your health care plan, period. No one will take it away, no matter what.

Barack Obama

And we can see the positive impacts right here at Solyndra. Less than a year ago, we were standing on what was an empty lot.But through the Recovery Act, this company received a loan to expand its operations. This new factory is the result of those loans.

Barack Obama

And we have done more in the two and a half years that I've been in here than the previous 43 Presidents to uphold that principle, whether it's ending 'don't ask, don't tell,' making sure that gay and lesbian partners can visit each other in hospitals, making sure that federal benefits can be provided to same-sex couples.

Barack Obama

Are we a nation that educates the world's best and brightest in our universities, only to send them home to create businesses in countries that compete against us? Or are we a nation that encourages them to stay and create jobs, businesses, and industries right here in America?

Barack Obama

As I said last week in the wake of the grand jury decision, I think Ferguson laid bare a problem that is not unique to St. Louis or that area, and is not unique to our time, and that is a simmering distrust that exists between too many police departments and too many communities of color.

Barack Obama

As I've said, there were patriots who supported this war, and patriots who opposed it. And all of us are united in appreciation for our servicemen and women, and our hopes for Iraqis' future.

Barack Obama

As a nuclear power - as the only nuclear power to have used a nuclear weapon - the United States has a moral responsibility to act.

Barack Obama

As president, I'm committed to making Washington work better and rebuilding the trust of the people who sent us here.

Barack Obama

Building new roads and bridges creates jobs. Growing our exports creates jobs. Reforming our outdated tax system and our broken immigration system creates jobs.

Barack Obama

But do I think that our actions in anyway violate the War Powers Resolution, the answer is no.

Barack Obama

But if you - if what - the reports are true, what they're saying is, is that as a consequence of us getting 30 million additional people health care, at the margins that's going to increase our costs, we knew that.

Barack Obama

But let me perfectly clear, because I know you'll hear the same old claims that rolling back these tax breaks means a massive tax increase on the American people: if your family earns less than $250,000 a year, you will not see your taxes increased a single dime. I repeat: not one single dime.

Barack Obama

But what we can do, as flawed as we are, is still see God in other people, and do our best to help them find their own grace. That's what I strive to do, that's what I pray to do every day.

Barack Obama

Change will not come if we wait for some other person or some other time. We are the ones we've been waiting for. We are the change that we seek.

Barack Obama

Community colleges play an important role in helping people transition between careers by providing the retooling they need to take on a new career.

Barack Obama

Contrary to the claims of some of my critics and some of the editorial pages, I am an ardent believer in the free market.

Barack Obama

Cutting the deficit by gutting our investments in innovation and education is like lightening an overloaded airplane by removing its engine. It may make you feel like you're flying high at first, but it won't take long before you feel the impact.

Barack Obama

Even when folks are hitting you over the head, you can't stop marching. Even when they're turning the hoses on you, you can't stop.

Barack Obama

Focusing your life solely on making a buck shows a certain poverty of ambition. It asks too little of yourself. Because it's only when you hitch your wagon to something larger than yourself that you realize your true potential.

Barack Obama

For more than four decades, the Libyan people have been ruled by a tyrant - Moammar Gaddafi. He has denied his people freedom, exploited their wealth, murdered opponents at home and abroad, and terrorized innocent people around the world - including Americans who were killed by Libyan agents.

Barack Obama

Four years ago, I promised to end the war in Iraq. We did. I promised to refocus on the terrorists who actually attacked us on 9/11. We have. We've blunted the Taliban's momentum in Afghanistan, and in 2014, our longest war will be over. A new tower rises above the New York skyline, al Qaeda is on the path to defeat, and Osama bin Laden is dead.

Barack Obama

Here at this site, Solyndra expects to make enough solar panels each year to generate 500 megawatts of electricity. And over the lifetime of this expanded facility, that could be like replacing as many as eight coal-fired power plants.

Barack Obama

I am the commander in chief of the United States armed forces, and Iraq is gonna have to ultimately provide for its own security.

Barack Obama

I believe in American exceptionalism, just as I suspect that the Brits believe in British exceptionalism and the Greeks believe in Greek exceptionalism.

Barack Obama

I believe marriage is between a man and a woman. I am not in favor of gay marriage. But when you start playing around with constitutions, just to prohibit somebody who cares about another person, it just seems to me that's not what America's about. Usually, our constitutions expand liberties, they don't contract them.

Barack Obama

I can make a firm pledge, under my plan, no family making less than $250,000 a year will see any form of tax increase.

Not your income tax, not your payroll tax, not your capital gains taxes, not any of your taxes.

Barack Obama

I cannot swallow whole the view of Lincoln as the Great Emancipator.

Barack Obama

I consider it part of my responsibility as President of the United States to fight against negative stereotypes of Islam wherever they appear.

Barack Obama

I don't care whether you're driving a hybrid or an SUV. If you're headed for a cliff, you have to change direction. That's what the American people called for in November, and that's what we intend to deliver.

Barack Obama

I don't oppose all wars. What I am opposed to is a dumb war. What I am opposed to is a rash war.

Barack Obama

I don't think marriage is a civil right, but I think that being able to transfer property is a civil right.

Barack Obama

I found this national debt, doubled, wrapped in a big bow waiting for me as I stepped into the Oval Office.

Barack Obama

I have Muslim members of my family. I have lived in Muslim countries.

Barack Obama

I just miss - I miss being anonymous.

Barack Obama

I just want to go through Central Park and watch folks passing by. Spend the whole day watching people. I miss that.

Barack Obama

I know my country has not perfected itself. At times, we've struggled to keep the promise of liberty and equality for all of our people. We've made our share of mistakes, and there are times when our actions around the world have not lived up to our best intentions.

Barack Obama

I know that campaigns can seem small, and even silly. Trivial things become big distractions. Serious issues become sound bites. And the truth gets buried under an avalanche of money and advertising. If you're sick of hearing me approve this message, believe me - so am I.

Barack Obama

I know that there are millions of Americans who are content with their health care coverage - they like their plan and, most importantly, they value their relationship with their doctor.

Barack Obama

I mean, I do think at a certain point you've made enough money.

Barack Obama

I miss Saturday morning, rolling out of bed, not shaving, getting into my car with my girls, driving to the supermarket, squeezing the fruit, getting my car washed, taking walks.

Barack Obama

I opposed the Defense of Marriage Act in 1996. It should be repealed and I will vote for its repeal on the Senate floor. I will also oppose any proposal to amend the U.S. Constitution to ban gays and lesbians from marrying.

Barack Obama

I said that America's role would be limited; that we would not put ground troops into Libya; that we would focus our unique capabilities on the front end of the operation, and that we would transfer responsibility to our allies and partners.

Barack Obama

I think it is important for Europe to understand that even though I am president and George Bush is not president, Al Qaeda is still a threat.

Barack Obama

I think one of the great things about the United States has been our ability to maintain a distinction between our military and domestic law enforcement.

Barack Obama

I think same sex couples should be able to get married.

Barack Obama

I think that there's no doubt that as I see friends, families, children of gay couples who are thriving, you know, that has an impact on how I think about these issues.

Barack Obama

I think there are a whole host of things that are civil rights, and then there are other things - such as traditional marriage - that, I think, express a community's concern and regard for a particular institution.

Barack Obama

I think what you're seeing is a profound recognition on the part of the American people that gays and lesbians and transgender persons are our brothers, our sisters, our children, our cousins, our friends, our co-workers, and that they've got to be treated like every other American. And I think that principle will win out.

Barack Obama

I think when you spread the wealth around it's good for everybody.

Barack Obama

I want to be very clear: I will not sign on to any health plan that adds to our deficits over the next decade.

Barack Obama

I want to reform the tax code so that it's simple, fair, and asks the wealthiest households to pay higher taxes on incomes over $250,000 - the same rate we had when Bill Clinton was president; the same rate we had when our economy created nearly 23 million new jobs, the biggest surplus in history, and a lot of millionaires to boot.

Barack Obama

I will continue to believe that Israel's security is paramount.

Barack Obama

I will cut taxes - cut taxes - for 95 percent of all working families, because, in an economy like this, the last thing we should do is raise taxes on the middle class.

Barack Obama

I will never turn Medicare into a voucher. No American should ever have to spend their golden years at the mercy of insurance companies. They should retire with the care and dignity they have earned.

Barack Obama

I would put our legislative and foreign policy accomplishments in our first two years against any president - with the possible exceptions of Johnson, FDR, and Lincoln - just in terms of what we've gotten done in modern history. But, you know, but when it comes to the economy, we've got a lot more work to do. And we're gonna keep on at it.

Barack Obama

I'm a Christian by choice.

Barack Obama

I'm a warrior for the middle class.

Barack Obama

I'm going to try to unite all Americans.

Barack Obama

I'm no longer just a candidate. I'm the President. I know what it means to send young Americans into battle, for I have held in my arms the mothers and fathers of those who didn't return. I've shared the pain of families who've lost their homes, and the frustration of workers who've lost their jobs.

Barack Obama

I'm the president of the United States. I'm not the emperor of the United States.

Barack Obama

I've been fighting with Acorn, alongside Acorn, on issues you care about, my entire career.

Barack Obama

I've got a pen and I've got a phone - and I can use that pen to sign executive orders and take executive actions and administrative actions that move the ball forward.

Barack Obama

I've got two daughters. 9 years old and 6 years old. I am going to teach them first of all about values and morals. But if they make a mistake, I don't want them punished with a baby.

Barack Obama

I've said very clearly, including in a State of the Union address, that I'm against 'don't ask, don't tell' and that we're going to end this policy.

Barack Obama

If everybody that voted in 2008 shows up in 2010, we will win this election. We will win this election.

Barack Obama

If people continue to feel like Democrats are looking after poor folks and Republicans are looking after rich folks and nobody is looking after me, then we don't get a lot of stuff done. And the trend lines evidence the fact that folks have gotten squeezed. And obviously, 2007, 2008 really ripped open for people how vulnerable they were.

Barack Obama

If the critics are right that I've made all my decisions based on polls, then I must not be very good at reading them.

Barack Obama

If the people cannot trust their government to do the job for which it exists - to protect them and to promote their common welfare - all else is lost.

Barack Obama

If we choose to keep those tax breaks for millionaires and billionaires, if we choose to keep a tax break for corporate jet owners, if we choose to keep tax breaks for oil and gas companies that are making hundreds of billions of dollars, then that means we've got to cut some kids off from getting a college scholarship.

Barack Obama

If you were successful, somebody along the line gave you some help... Somebody helped to create this unbelievable American system that we have that allowed you to thrive. Somebody invested in roads and bridges. If you've got a business - you didn't build that. Somebody else made that happen.

Barack Obama

If you're looking for the safe choice, you shouldn't be supporting a black guy named Barack Obama to be the next leader of the free world.

Barack Obama

If you're walking down the right path and you're willing to keep walking, eventually you'll make progress.

Barack Obama

In America, there's a failure to appreciate Europe's leading role in the world.

Barack Obama

In December, I agreed to extend the tax cuts for the wealthiest Americans because it was the only way I could prevent a tax hike on middle-class Americans. But we cannot afford $1 trillion worth of tax cuts for every millionaire and billionaire in our society. We can't afford it. And I refuse to renew them again.

Barack Obama

In a summer marked by instability in the Middle East and Eastern Europe, I know the world also took notice of the small American city of Ferguson, Missouri - where a young man was killed, and a community was divided. So yes, we have our own racial and ethnic tensions.

Barack Obama

In a world of complex threats, our security and leadership depends on all elements of our power - including strong and principled diplomacy.

Barack Obama

In fact, the best thing we could do on taxes for all Americans is to simplify the individual tax code. This will be a tough job, but members of both parties have expressed an interest in doing this, and I am prepared to join them.

Barack Obama

In the absence of sound oversight,responsible businesses are forced to compete against unscrupulous and underhanded businesses, who are unencumbered by any restrictions on activities that might harm the environment, or take advantage of middle-class families, or threaten to bring down the entire financial system.

Barack Obama

In the end, that's what this election is about. Do we participate in a politics of cynicism or a politics of hope?

Barack Obama

In the white community, the path to a more perfect union means acknowledging that what ails the African-American community does not just exist in the minds of black people; that the legacy of discrimination - and current incidents of discrimination, while less overt than in the past - are real and must be addressed.

Barack Obama

In too many communities, too many young men of color are left behind and seen only as objects of fear. Through initiatives like My Brother's Keeper, I'm personally committed to changing both perception and reality.

Barack Obama

Issues are never simple. One thing I'm proud of is that very rarely will you hear me simplify the issues.

Barack Obama

It took a lot of blood, sweat and tears to get to where we are today, but we have just begun. Today we begin in earnest the work of making sure that the world we leave our children is just a little bit better than the one we inhabit today.

Barack Obama

It was not a religion that attacked us that September day. It was al-Qaeda. We will not sacrifice the liberties we cherish or hunker down behind walls of suspicion and mistrust.

Barack Obama

It was the labor movement that helped secure so much of what we take for granted today. The 40-hour work week, the minimum wage, family leave, health insurance, Social Security, Medicare, retirement plans. The cornerstones of the middle-class security all bear the union label.

Barack Obama

It's not enough to train today's workforce. We also have to prepare tomorrow's workforce by guaranteeing every child access to a world-class education.

Barack Obama

It's not surprising, then, they get bitter, they cling to guns or religion or antipathy to people who aren't like them or anti-immigrant sentiment or anti-trade sentiment as a way to explain their frustrations.

Barack Obama

It's time to fundamentally change the way that we do business in Washington. To help build a new foundation for the 21st century, we need to reform our government so that it is more efficient, more transparent, and more creative. That will demand new thinking and a new sense of responsibility for every dollar that is spent.

Barack Obama

John Kerry believes in an America where hard work is rewarded.

Barack Obama

Let me be absolutely clear. Israel is a strong friend of Israel's. It will be a strong friend of Israel's under a McCain administration. It will be a strong friend of Israel's under an Obama administration. So that policy is not going to change.

Barack Obama

Let me even say before I even get inaugurated, during the transition we are going to be having meetings all across the country with community organizations so that you have input into the agenda for the next presidency of the United States of America.

Barack Obama

Let us remember we are all part of one American family. We are united in common values, and that includes belief in equality under the law, basic respect for public order, and the right of peaceful protest.

Barack Obama

Let's be honest - tracking down, rounding up, and deporting millions of people isn't realistic. Anyone who suggests otherwise isn't being straight with you. It's also not who we are as Americans.

Barack Obama

Michelle and I don't want anyone telling us who our family's doctor should be - and no one should decide that for you either. Under our proposals, if you like your doctor, you keep your doctor. If you like your current insurance, you keep that insurance. Period, end of story.

Barack Obama

Millions of us, myself included, go back generations in this country, with ancestors who put in the painstaking work to become citizens. So we don't like the notion that anyone might get a free pass to American citizenship.

Barack Obama

Money is not the only answer, but it makes a difference.

Barack Obama

My family, frankly, they weren't folks who went to church every week. My mother was one of the most spiritual people I knew but she didn't raise me in the church, so I came to my Christian faith later in life and it was because the precepts of Jesus Christ spoke to me in terms of the kind of life that I would want to lead.

Barack Obama

My fellow Americans, we are and always will be a nation of immigrants. We were strangers once, too.

Barack Obama

My job is not to represent Washington to you, but to represent you to Washington.

Barack Obama

My parents shared not only an improbable love, they shared an abiding faith in the possibilities of this nation. They would give me an African name, Barack, or blessed, believing that in a tolerant America your name is no barrier to success.

Barack Obama

My task over the last two years hasn't just been to stop the bleeding. My task has also been to try to figure out how do we address some of the structural problems in the economy that have prevented more Googles from being created.

Barack Obama

No other country in the world does what we do. On every issue, the world turns to us, not simply because of the size of our economy or our military might - but because of the ideals we stand for, and the burdens we bear to advance them.

Barack Obama

No party has a monopoly on wisdom. No democracy works without compromise. But when Governor Romney and his allies in Congress tell us we can somehow lower our deficit by spending trillions more on new tax breaks for the wealthy - well, you do the math. I refuse to go along with that. And as long as I'm President, I never will.

Barack Obama

Nobody wants to put the creditworthiness of the United States in jeopardy. Nobody wants to see the United States default. So we've got to seize this moment, and we have to seize it soon.

Barack Obama

Now we're in the midst of not just advocating for change, not just calling for change - we're doing the grinding, sometimes frustrating work of delivering change - inch by inch, day by day.

Barack Obama

Now you have a choice: we can give more tax breaks to corporations that ship jobs overseas, or we can start rewarding companies that open new plants and train new workers and create new jobs here, in the United States of America.

Barack Obama

Now, anybody who thinks that we can move this economy forward with just a few folks at the top doing well, hoping that it's going to trickle down to working people who are running faster and faster just to keep up, you'll never see it.

Barack Obama

Now, as a nation, we don't promise equal outcomes, but we were founded on the idea everybody should have an equal opportunity to succeed. No matter who you are, what you look like, where you come from, you can make it. That's an essential promise of America. Where you start should not determine where you end up.

Barack Obama

Of course, there is no question that Libya - and the world - will be better off with Gaddafi out of power. I, along with many other world leaders, have embraced that goal, and will actively pursue it through non-military means. But broadening our military mission to include regime change would be a mistake.

Barack Obama

Of course, violence will not end with our combat mission. Extremists will continue to set off bombs, attack Iraqi civilians and try to spark sectarian strife. But ultimately, these terrorists will fail to achieve their goals.

Barack Obama

On every front there are clear answers out there that can make this country stronger, but we're going to break through the fear and the frustration people are feeling. Our job is to make sure that even as we make progress, that we are also giving people a sense of hope and vision for the future.

Barack Obama

One of the great strengths of the United States is... we have a very large Christian population - we do not consider ourselves a Christian nation or a Jewish nation or a Muslim nation. We consider ourselves a nation of citizens who are bound by ideals and a set of values.

Barack Obama

Operations in Iraq and Afghanistan and the war on terrorism have reduced the pace of military transformation and have revealed our lack of preparation for defensive and stability operations. This Administration has overextended our military.

Barack Obama

Our combat mission is ending, but our commitment to Iraq's future is not.

Barack Obama

Our friends at the Republican convention were more than happy to talk about everything they think is wrong with

America, but they didn't have much to say about how they'd make it right. They want your vote, but they don't want you to know their plan.

Barack Obama

Our higher education system is one of the things that makes America exceptional. There's no place else that has the assets we do when it comes to higher education. People from all over the world aspire to come here and study here. And that is a good thing.

Barack Obama

Our priority is to go after ISIL. And so what we have said is that we are not engaging in a military action against the Syrian regime. We are going after ISIL facilities and personnel who are using Syria as a safe haven, in service of our strategy in Iraq.

Barack Obama

Ours is a nation of laws: of citizens who live under them and for the citizens who enforce them. So, to a community in Ferguson that is rightly hurting and looking for answers, let me call once again for us to seek some understanding rather than simply holler at each other. Let's seek to heal rather than to wound each other.

Barack Obama

Over the last 15 months, we've traveled to every corner of the United States. I've now been in 57 states? I think one left to go.

Barack Obama

Part of the reason that our politics seems so tough right now and facts and science and argument does not seem to be winning the day all the time is because we're hardwired not to always think clearly when we're scared. And the country's scared.

Barack Obama

People of Berlin - people of the world - this is our moment. This is our time.

Barack Obama

Since I'm the president and Democrats have controlled the House and the Senate, it's understandable that people are saying, you know, 'What have you done?'

Barack Obama

So long as I'm Commander-in-Chief, we will sustain the strongest military the world has ever known. When you take off the uniform, we will serve you as well as you've served us - because no one who fights for this country should have to fight for a job, or a roof over their head, or the care that they need when they come home.

Barack Obama

So while I will never minimize the costs involved in military action, I am convinced that a failure to act in Libya would have carried a far greater price for America.

Barack Obama

So while an incredible amount of progress has been made, on this fifth anniversary, I wanted to come here and tell the people of this city directly: My administration is going to stand with you - and fight alongside you - until the job is done. Until New Orleans is all the way back, all the way.

Barack Obama

Take off your bedroom slippers. Put on your marching shoes,' he said, his voice rising as applause and cheers mounted. 'Shake it off. Stop complainin'. Stop grumblin'. Stop cryin'. We are going to press on. We have work to do.

Barack Obama

That's the good thing about being president, I can do whatever I want.

Barack Obama

The Bush Administration's failure to be consistently involved in helping Israel achieve peace with the Palestinians has been both wrong for our friendship with Israel, as well as badly damaging to our standing in the Arab world.

Barack Obama

The Internet didn't get invented on its own. Government research created the Internet so that all the companies could make money off the Internet. The point is, is that when we succeed, we succeed because of our individual initiative, but also because we do things together.

Barack Obama

The Middle East is obviously an issue that has plagued the region for centuries.

Barack Obama

The United States has been enriched by Muslim Americans. Many other Americans have Muslims in their families or have lived in a Muslim-majority country - I know, because I am one of them.

Barack Obama

The United States is not, and never will be, at war with Islam.

Barack Obama

The day I'm inaugurated, this country looks at itself differently and the world looks at America differently. If you believe that we've got to heal America and we've got to repair our standing in the world, then I think my supporters believe that I am a messenger who can deliver that message around the world in a way that no other candidate can do.

Barack Obama

The fact that my 15 minutes of fame has extended a little longer than 15 minutes is somewhat surprising to me and completely baffling to my wife.

Barack Obama

The fact that we are here today to debate raising America's debt limit is a sign of leadership failure. America has a debt problem and a failure of leadership. Americans deserve better. I, therefore, intend to oppose the effort to increase America's debt.

Barack Obama

The future rewards those who press on. I don't have time to feel sorry for myself. I don't have time to complain. I'm going to press on.

Barack Obama

The immigration issue is, I recognize, one that generates a lot of passion, but it does not make sense for us to want to push talent out.

Barack Obama

The last thing you want to do is raise taxes in the middle of the recession because that would just suck up and take more demand out of the economy and put businesses in a further hole.

Barack Obama

The shift to a cleaner energy economy wont happen overnight, and it will require tough choices along the way. But the debate is settled. Climate change is a fact.

Barack Obama

The thing about hip-hop today is it's smart, it's insightful. The way they can communicate a complex message in a very short space is remarkable.

Barack Obama

There are millions of Americans outside Washington who are tired of stale political arguments and are moving this country forward. They believe, and I believe, that here in America, our success should depend not on accident of birth, but the strength of our work ethic and the scope of our dreams.

Barack Obama

There are patriots who opposed the war in Iraq and there are patriots who supported the war in Iraq. We are one people, all of us pledging allegiance to the stars and stripes, all of us defending the United States of America.

Barack Obama

There is not a liberal America and a conservative America - there is the United States of America. There is not a black America and a white America and latino America and asian America - there's the United States of America.

Barack Obama

There is probably a perverse pride in my administration... that we were going to do the right thing, even if short-term it was unpopular. And I think anybody who's occupied this office has to remember that success is determined by an intersection in policy and politics and that you can't be neglecting of marketing and P.R. and public opinion.

Barack Obama

There's not a liberal America and a conservative America - there's the United States of America.

Barack Obama

This is the moment when we must build on the wealth that open markets have created, and share its benefits more equitably. Trade has been a cornerstone of our growth and global development. But we will not be able to sustain this growth if it favors the few, and not the many.

Barack Obama

This is the moment when we must come together to save this planet. Let us resolve that we will not leave our children a world where the oceans rise and famine spreads and terrible storms devastate our lands.

Barack Obama

Those who oppose reform will also tell you that under our plan, you won't get to choose your doctor - that some bureaucrat will choose for you. That's also not true.

Barack Obama

To avoid being mistaken for a sellout, I chose my friends carefully. The more politically active black students. The foreign students. The Chicanos. The Marxist professors and structural feminists and punk-rock performance poets.

Barack Obama

Today we are engaged in a deadly global struggle for those who would intimidate, torture, and murder people for exercising the most basic freedoms. If we are to win this struggle and spread those freedoms, we must keep our own moral compass pointed in a true direction.

Barack Obama

Tonight, we gather to affirm the greatness of our nation - not because of the height of our skyscrapers, or the power of our military, or the size of our economy. Our pride is based on a very simple premise, summed up in a declaration made over two hundred years ago.

Barack Obama

Trayvon Martin could have been me 35 years ago.

Barack Obama

Understand, our police officers put their lives on the line for us every single day. They've got a tough job to do to maintain public safety and hold accountable those who break the law.

Barack Obama

Unlike my opponent, I will not let oil companies write this country's energy plan, or endanger our coastlines, or collect another $4 billion in corporate welfare from our taxpayers.

Barack Obama

We all knew this. We all knew that it would take more time than any of us want to dig ourselves out of this hole created by this economic crisis.

Barack Obama

We all remember Abraham Lincoln as the leader who saved our Union. Founder of the Republican Party.

Barack Obama

We are not at war against Islam.

Barack Obama

We can choose a future where we export more products and outsource fewer jobs. After a decade that was defined by what we bought and borrowed, we're getting back to basics, and doing what America has always done best: We're making things again.

Barack Obama

We can't drive our SUVs and eat as much as we want and keep our homes on 72 degrees at all times... and then just expect that other countries are going to say OK. That's not leadership. That's not going to happen.

Barack Obama

We can't get to the $4 trillion in savings that we need by just cutting the 12 percent of the budget that pays for things like medical research and education funding and food inspectors and the weather service. And we can't just do it by making seniors pay more for Medicare.

Barack Obama

We can't have special interests sitting shotgun. We gotta have middle class families up in front. We don't mind the Republicans joining us. They can come for the ride, but they gotta sit in back.

Barack Obama

We cannot continue to rely only on our military in order to achieve the national security objectives that we've set. We've got to have a civilian national security force that's just as powerful, just as strong, just as well-funded.

Barack Obama

We didn't become the most prosperous country in the world just by rewarding greed and recklessness. We didn't come this far by letting the special interests run wild. We didn't do it just by gambling and chasing paper profits on Wall Street. We built this country by making things, by producing goods we could sell.

Barack Obama

We have an obligation and a responsibility to be investing in our students and our schools. We must make sure that people who have the grades, the desire and the will, but not the money, can still get the best education possible.

Barack Obama

We have now just enshrined, as soon as I sign this bill, the core principle that everybody should have some basic security when it comes to their healthcare.

Barack Obama

We have real enemies in the world. These enemies must be found. They must be pursued and they must be defeated.

Barack Obama

We know that the nation that goes all-in on innovation today will own the global economy tomorrow. This is an edge America cannot surrender.

Barack Obama

We need earmark reform, and when I'm President, I will go line by line to make sure that we are not spending money unwisely.

Barack Obama

We need somebody who's got the heart, the empathy, to recognize what it's like to be a young teenage mom, the empathy to understand what it's like to be poor or African-American or gay or disabled or old - and that's the criterion by which I'll be selecting my judges.

Barack Obama

We need to internalize this idea of excellence. Not many folks spend a lot of time trying to be excellent.

Barack Obama

We need to recognize that the situation in Ferguson speaks to broader challenges that we still face as a nation. The fact is, in too many parts of this country, a deep distrust exists between law enforcement and communities of color. Some of this is the result of the legacy of racial discrimination in this country.

Barack Obama

We need to steer clear of this poverty of ambition, where people want to drive fancy cars and wear nice clothes and live in nice apartments but don't want to work hard to accomplish these things. Everyone should try to realize their full potential.

Barack Obama

We proved that we are still a people capable of doing big things and tackling our biggest challenges.

Barack Obama

We want everybody to act like adults, quit playing games, realize that it's not just my way or the highway.

Barack Obama

We welcome the scrutiny of the world - because what you see in America is a country that has steadily worked to address our problems and make our union more perfect.

Barack Obama

We will keep the promise of Social Security by taking the responsible steps to strengthen it - not by turning it over to Wall Street.

Barack Obama

We worship an awesome God in the Blue States, and we don't like federal agents poking around our libraries in the Red States. We coach Little League in the Blue States and have gay friends in the Red States.

Barack Obama

We're not going to baby sit a civil war.

Barack Obama

We've persevered because of a belief we share with the Iraqi people - a belief that out of the ashes of war, a new beginning could be born in this cradle of civilization. Through this remarkable chapter in the history of the United States and Iraq, we have met our responsibility. Now, it's time to turn the page.

Barack Obama

We've protected thousands of people in Libya; we have not seen a single U.S. casualty; there's no risks of additional escalation. This operation is limited in time and in scope.

Barack Obama

We, the People, recognize that we have responsibilities as well as rights; that our destinies are bound together; that a freedom which only asks what's in it for me, a freedom without a commitment to others, a freedom without love or charity or duty or patriotism, is unworthy of our founding ideals, and those who died in their defense.

Barack Obama

What I believe is that marriage is between a man and a woman, but what I also believe is that we have an obligation to make sure that gays and lesbians have the rights of citizenship that afford them visitations to hospitals, that allow them to be, to transfer property between partners, to make certain that they're not discriminated on the job.

Barack Obama

What I believe unites the people of this nation, regardless of race or region or party, young or old, rich or poor, is the simple, profound belief in opportunity for all - the notion that if you work hard and take responsibility, you can get ahead.

Barack Obama

What I think is fair to say is that, coming out of the Republican camp, there have been efforts to suggest that perhaps I'm not who I say I am when it comes to my faith - something which I find deeply offensive, and that has been going on for a pretty long time.

Barack Obama

What I worry about would be that you essentially have two chambers, the House and the Senate, but you have simply, majoritarian, absolute power on either side. And that's just not what the founders intended.

Barack Obama

What Washington needs is adult supervision.

Barack Obama

What do you think a stimulus is? It's spending - that's the whole point! Seriously.

Barack Obama

What is a danger is that we stay stuck in a new normal where unemployment rates stay high, people who have jobs see their incomes go up, businesses make big profits. But they're learned to do more with less, and so they don't hire.

Barack Obama

What makes us Americans is our shared commitment to an ideal - that all of us are created equal, and all of us have the chance to make of our lives what we will.

Barack Obama

When BP was not moving fast enough on claims, we told BP to set aside $20 billion in a fund - managed by an independent third party - to help all those whose lives have been turned upside down by the spill.

Barack Obama

When states like Alabama and Arizona passed some of the harshest immigration laws in history, my Attorney General took them on in court and we won.

Barack Obama

When we think of the major threats to our national security, the first to come to mind are nuclear proliferation, rogue states and global terrorism. But another kind of threat lurks beyond our shores, one from nature, not humans - an avian flu pandemic.

Barack Obama

Where the stakes are the highest, in the war on terror, we cannot possibly succeed without extraordinary international cooperation. Effective international police actions require the highest degree of intelligence sharing, planning and collaborative enforcement.

Barack Obama

Whether our forebears were strangers who crossed the Atlantic or the Pacific or the Rio Grande, we are here only because this country welcomed them in and taught them that to be an American is about something more than what we look like, or what our last names are, or how we worship.

Barack Obama

While I understand the passions and the anger that arise over the death of Michael Brown, giving into that anger by looting or carrying guns, and even attacking the police, only serves to raise tensions and stir chaos.

Barack Obama

Why can't I just eat my waffle?

Barack Obama

With patient and firm determination, I am going to press on for jobs. I'm going to press on for equality. I'm going to press on for the sake of our children. I'm going to press on for the sake of all those families who are struggling right now. I don't have time to feel sorry for myself. I don't have time to complain. I am going to press on.

Barack Obama

With the changing economy, no one has lifetime employment. But community colleges provide lifetime employability.

Barack Obama

You can choose a future where more Americans have the chance to gain the skills they need to compete, no matter how old they are or how much money they have. Education was the gateway to opportunity for me. It was the gateway for Michelle. And now more than ever, it is the gateway to a middle-class life.

Barack Obama

You have young men of color in many communities who are more likely to end up in jail or in the criminal justice system than they are in a good job or in college. And, you know, part of my job, that I can do, I think, without any potential conflicts, is to get at those root causes.

Barack Obama

You know, my faith is one that admits some doubt.

Barack Obama

You know, one of the things I think you understand as president is you're held responsible for everything, but you don't always have control of everything, right?

Barack Obama

This page is intentionally left blank

This page is intentionally left blank

This page is intentionally left blank

This page is intentionally left blank

This page is intentionally left blank

www.ingramcontent.com/pod-product-compliance
Lightning Source LLC
Chambersburg PA
CBHW071121280526
45787CB00003B/1124